Software Licensing Agreements - What You Need To Know About Software Licenses

A Quick Legal Guide

By Mike Young, Esq.

Copyright Notice

For more information, please read the "*Disclosures and Disclaimers*" section at the end of this guide.

First Print Edition, February 2019

Published by Internet Attorneys Association LLC (the "Publisher").

Table of Contents

How To Use This Guide

Each Quick Legal Guide is designed as a resource to quickly learn the most important things you need to know about one business legal topic.

In the *Introduction* section we'll define the meaning of "software license" as the term is used in this guide.

In *Chapter 1*, we'll cover the scope of a software license. In other words, the key terms the licensor can use to determine how broad or narrow the permission(s) received by the licensee will be.

Then we'll identify and discuss popular types of software licenses in *Chapter 2*.

In *Chapter 3*, we'll discuss the important role open source licensing plays in both free and paid software.

Public domain software is discussed in *Chapter 4*. Although public domain software isn't licensed, knowing whether part of a software's source code[1] is or isn't in the public domain is important.

---

[1] Source code is the text of the software's programming language telling the computer what to do. It usually contains

In *Chapter 5*, we'll put it all together so you know how to create a software license that's right for you.

The guide also contains a *Quick Start Checklist* so you know what to do after reading the guide.

Additional material, including a *Resources* section, is located at the back of this guide. These reference materials should be used as-needed but aren't essential to understanding the topic.

---

comments from the developer(s) about what each part of the code does.

Introduction - What Is A Software License?

Before we get started, let's define "software license" so that we're working off of the same page.

In short, a "software license" is a grant of permission by the owner of a legal right to software (a "licensor") for another person or entity (the "licensee") *to do something* with that software.

Equally important, the license tells the licensee what it *cannot do* with the software.

Let's get started in the first chapter by learning how to customize the permission granted by a software license to meet your needs.

Chapter 1 - Scope of License

The scope of the license granted by the licensor determines what a licensee can and cannot do with the software.

For example, an end user license agreement (EULA) will let the licensee use the software but would not allow the licensee to sublicense the software to others for use.

The typical license scope will be defined by a *combination* of the following variables:

- Perpetual or Non-Perpetual
- Irrevocable or Revocable
- Exclusive or Non-Exclusive
- Transferable or Non-Transferable
- Assignable or Non-Assignable
- Sublicensable or Non-Sublicensable.

Perpetual or Non-Perpetual License

A *perpetual* license is permanent in the sense that the licensee has the ongoing rights granted by the license unless the licensee violates the terms or conditions.

In contrast, a *non-perpetual* license is time-limited instead of permanent. The amount of time the software is licensed will vary.

For instance, a popular non-perpetual license is a monthly subscription Software-as-a-Service (SaaS) license for cloud-based software. If the licensee doesn't pay the monthly fee, the license terminates and the licensee no longer has the right to use the software.

On the other hand, it's common for licensing of complex software to be part of a longer-term agreement (e.g. 1, 2, 5 or more years).
These longer-term agreements are often customized for each licensee and may also include things like upgrades to new versions of the software and maintenance provisions where the licensor provides services to make sure the software is running the way the licensee wants.

Whether a license is *perpetual* or *non-perpetual*, it typically has provisions that terminate the license because of licensee misconduct.

For example, a EULA would let the licensee use the software for as long as the licensee wants to. However, if the licensee decided to sell bootleg[2] copies of the software to others, the "permanent" license would terminate because the licensee didn't have the right to sell copies of software the licensee was only entitled to use.

Some licenses also provide for termination if a major event occurs, such as death of an individual licensee or the licensee files for bankruptcy.

Irrevocable or Revocable License

Irrevocable software licenses are about as rare as unicorns. As mentioned previously, even perpetual licenses usually have provisions that will terminate the license because of licensee misconduct.

When looking at a license, you should assume it's *revocable* and identify the provisions that will cause it to terminate. For example, non-payment of a recurring licensing fee, licensee misconduct, a specific end date stated in the license, etc.

---

[2] Bootleg software is an illegal unauthorized copy.

Even if the license says it's irrevocable, there's probably one or more clauses that provide for it to be revoked by the licensor. For example, if a licensee starts selling bootleg copies of the software to others, the license will probably provide for termination.

Exclusive or Non-Exclusive License

A license can be *exclusive* in the sense the licensor is granting the license to one licensee. Or it can be granted exclusively to one licensee within a particular field (e.g. pharmaceutical sales) or a geographic area (e.g. an exclusive license for use in the State of Texas).

As a general rule, most licenses are *non-exclusive.* In other words, the licensor can sell (or give away) as many licenses as the licensor wants.

There's often a premium charged for an *exclusive* license to make up for revenues the licensor will lose from not being able to sell licenses to others.

Transferable or Non-Transferable License

A *transferable* license is one the licensee can transfer to a third party. Upon transfer, the third party assumes all of the rights and responsibilities as the new licensee. The original license recipient is no longer a licensee.

For example, the owner of a transferable license sells his entire business. The license for the software is transferred to the buyer of the business (the new licensee) and the seller no longer has any rights to use it.

In contrast, a *non-transferable* license is one that cannot be transferred by the licensee to a third party.

However, it's common for licenses to state they are not transferable unless certain conditions are met (e.g. the licensor grants permission in writing for the transfer to occur).

Assignable or Non-Assignable License

An *assignable* software license is similar to a *transferable* license. A licensee might assign some or all of the licensee's rights and responsibilities under the license agreement to a third party (the assignee).

However, the license still exists between the licensor and the licensee.

This means the licensee is still responsible to the licensor for complying with the license. And the licensee is often liable to the licensor if the assignee violates the terms or conditions of the license.

For instance, let's say the licensee of customer relationship management (CRM) software decides to outsource customer support responsibilities to a third party. If permitted by the license, the licensee would assign some of its rights and responsibilities under the license to the third party so that party could use the CRM software to provide customer support.

However, the original licensor-licensee relationship is still in place, i.e. the licensee is still responsible to the licensor for complying with the license's terms and conditions. The assignment does not relieve the licensee of this responsibility.

Like *transferable* licenses, *assignable* licenses typically require the licensee to obtain prior written licensor consent to an assignment before it can be made.

Sublicensable or Non-Sublicensable License

A *sublicensable* license permits the licensee to issue a new license to a third party (a sublicensee) for some or all of the rights and responsibilities the licensee obtained under the original license.

This means there are two licenses: (1) the original license between licensor and licensee; and (2) a sublicense between the licensee and the sublicensee.

And like *transferable* licenses and *assignable* licenses, *sublicensable* licenses usually require the licensee to obtain prior written consent from the licensor to sublicense.

For instance, one might purchase a resale license. This resale license could provide the licensee the right to sublicense retail copies sold to customers with an end user license agreement (EULA).

Scope Limits On Licenses, Transfers, Assignments & Sublicenses

Whether it's a software license, license transfer, license assignment, or sublicense, one cannot sell or give away greater legal rights to others than one owns.

For example, a *non-exclusive monthly* licensee (e.g. a SaaS subscriber) cannot sell or give to another party an *exclusive perpetual* license. Why? Because the licensee does not possess an exclusive perpetual license.

Similarly, if a licensee has a *transferable EULA*, the licensee cannot transfer to a third party a license to sell multiple copies of the software to others as a retailer. Because a EULA doesn't give an end user such a resale right in the first place.

Chapter 2 - Popular Software License Types

The following is a brief overview of common software licensing agreements, including:

- Software Beta Testing Agreement
- Software Evaluation License Agreement
- End User License Agreement
- International Software Distribution License Agreement
- Mobile Application License Agreement
- Multi-User License Agreement
- Dual License Agreement
- Resale License Agreement
- Resell License Agreement
- Software-as-a-Service Agreement
- Software Development Agreement
- Software Escrow Agreement
- Software Trial License Agreement
- Hybrid Licensing Agreement

Software Beta Testing Agreement

Before releasing software to the public (or a new version of an existing software), it's common to have third parties "beta test" the software to identify bugs to be fixed and suggest improvements to the software.

Each of these beta testers are end users of non-retail software. This means the license will contain certain terms and conditions not seen in a standard EULA received by a purchaser after the software is released to the public.

Note that a beta testing agreement is not the same thing as a *Software Evaluation License Agreement.*

Software Evaluation License Agreement

A software evaluation license agreement is granted by the licensor to a prospective purchaser of the software for free or for a nominal fee (e.g. $5).

For a period of time (e.g. 30 days), the prospect can test the software to determine if it's something they want to purchase.

During the test period, the licensor may limit access to certain key features of the software as a means to encourage the prospect to buy[3]. The evaluation license will reflect this technical limitation.

End User License Agreement

An end user license agreement (EULA) is the most common type of license. As the name suggests, the license specifies what a software's actual user can and cannot do.

The rights granted by a licensor to an end user licensee are typically very restrictive, giving the licensee just enough permission to use the software but little else.

Note that sometimes the EULA is issued to a business entity where multiple employees are using the software under a single license. The entity itself is technically the end user.

In the alternative, the business entity may be granted a multi-user license with each individual employee receiving a separate EULA.

---

[3] An evaluation version of software is sometimes called a *demo version*. The "demo" is short for "demonstration."

International Software Distribution Licensing Agreement

To increase global sales, it's common for a software's owner to find foreign companies to distribute the software in other countries. This distribution agreement will be customized to reflect the type of licensing, including royalties or other payments by the foreign licensee to the licensor.

Many of these agreements are set up with a foreign company as a master licensee wholesaler with the ability to sublicense to others within the country as retail licensees. These retailers in turn sell the software to end users who receive EULAs.

Other distribution agreements are structured to have the foreign company sell directly as retailer in the country to the ultimate end users.

See *Resale License Agreement* below for more information.

Mobile Application License Agreement

A mobile application license is a type of EULA specifically tailored for software designed for mobile devices. These include cell phones and computer tablets.

In addition to the standard EULA provisions, these licenses must comply with the specific requirements of the mobile app stores (e.g. Google Play, Apple App Store, etc.) where they are sold.

And these mobile app licenses may have additional provisions to comply with privacy requirements related to user personal data (e.g. phone geolocation tracking).

Multi-User License Agreement

A multi-user license is a form of EULA that grants more than one person the right to use the software.

A simple multi-user license may grant a purchaser the right to have 2-3 people use the software.

You'll find more complex multi-user agreements where the licensee is a business entity. For example, there may be one company-wide license for all of the licensee's employees to use the software. Or the license may be restricted to a single site (e.g. all the workers in one office location).

Dual License Agreement

See *Hybrid Licensing Agreement* below.

Resale License Agreement

Sometimes a licensor will use a resale license agreement to authorize a licensee to resell software to others (resale rights).[4]

Three popular types of resale license agreements are:

(1) Resale License;
(2) *Master* Resale License; and
(3) *Private Label* Resale License.

Resale License

A standard *Resale License* typically lets the licensee resell the software as-is to third parties who receive a EULA.

---

[4] An *International Software Distribution Agreement* often contains a resale license.

Master Resale License

A *Master Resale License* grants the licensee the authority to sell *resale* rights to others. These buyers of resale licenses can then sell the software to others who receive a EULA. Note that a master resale licensee usually cannot sell *master resale* rights to others.

Private Label License

A *Private Label License* can be either a *Master Resale License* or a standard *Resale License*. In either case, the licensee has the right to rename/rebrand the software[5] before selling it to others.

However, a private label license rarely authorizes the recipient licensee to sell private label rights to others.

Note that each licensor cannot grant more rights than it has to others.

For example, the purchaser of a standard resale license for software cannot sell a master resale license to others.

---

[5] The ability to relabel or rebrand software is sometimes referred to as "white labeling."

Resell License Agreement

A common misspelling of *Resale License Agreement.* See above.

Software-as-a-Service Agreement

A Software-as-a-Service (SaaS) agreement grants the licensee permission to use an online software hosted on a cloud computing platform (e.g. Amazon AWS, Microsoft Azure, etc.).

SaaS licensing is often part of a subscription agreement (e.g. monthly membership agreement) where the license to use the software terminates when the licensee stops making recurring payments to access it. Yet it's common for SaaS licensing to be purchased with a single larger payment up front for "permanent" access instead of monthly or other periodic payments.

Although it may be described as permanent, in reality access will eventually be cut off for any number of reasons. For example, the software becomes obsolete and cannot be upgraded to match newer software sold by competitors. Or the licensor may go out of business.

SaaS licensing includes individual EULAs, multi-user licensing (often to companies for their employees), and even private label resale licensing where the SaaS is rebranded and sold on a different website by the resale licensee.

Software Development Agreement

A good software development agreement will identify who owns the software's intellectual property - (a) the client who paid for the software to be developed or (b) the developer who coded and possibly maintains the software.

If the agreement favors the client, the client will own all or most of the software's code. There may be no licensing.

On the other hand, it's common for a developer to retain ownership of code and license it to the client.

The scope of the license granted to the developer as licensor to the client as licensee is important for determining what the client can and cannot do with the software. For example, will the client receive a EULA or a broader license (e.g. one with resale rights)?

Some of the code used by the developer may be licensed from a third party. In such a case, the scope of the license granted by the developer to the client can't be broader in scope than the one the developer is relying upon to use the code in the first place. See *Chapter 3 - Open Source Licensing.*

Software Escrow Agreement

For expensive software, it's common for both the licensor and licensee to protect their respective interests using a software escrow agreement. The third-party escrow agent stores the source code that's being licensed.

The primary benefit to the licensor is that escrow prevents the licensee from violating the terms and conditions of the license by modifying the code, selling it to others, etc.

In addition, new versions of the software may be easily uploaded by the licensor to escrow as-needed during the term of the license. The licensor retains control of the modifications and it limits risk of intellectual property theft by the licensee during the upgrade process.

On the flip side, the escrow agreement protects the licensee too. For example, if the licensor files for bankruptcy, the escrow agent is usually authorized by the agreement to release the source code to the licensee so the software can continue to be used by the licensee even if the licensor's assets are liquidated because of insolvency.

Software Trial License Agreement

See *Software Evaluation License Agreement* above.

Hybrid Licensing Agreement

A hybrid licensing agreement (sometimes called a *Dual License Agreement)* contains multiple licenses to reflect different rights are being granted in a single agreement to the licensee.

This is common in software development agreements where the developer creates unique code but also relies upon code licensed from a third party (e.g. open source code) as part of software development.

The alternative to a hybrid licensing agreement is to have multiple license agreements to the licensee instead of a single agreement. A common risk with this approach is that the separate agreements are more likely to have conflicting terms and conditions than a single agreement describing all of the licensed rights.

Chapter 3 - Open Source Licensing

Open Source Code

Some code is distributed by open source licensing. These licenses generally encourage distribution of software where the licensee gets access to the source code.

See the *Resources* section at the end of this guide for popular source code repositories used for open source projects.

Common open source licenses (listed in alphabetical order) include:

- Apache License (v. 2.0)
- BSD (2-Clause and 3-Clause)
- Common Development and Distribution License
- Eclipse Public License (EPL)
- GNU (GPL and LGPL)
- MIT License
- Mozilla Public License (v. 2.0)

Many open source licenses require attribution (acknowledge where the code came from) by the licensee. In addition, licenses may favor the ability of licensees to modify code and share it as-modified with others.

Popular open source licenses are available online from the *Free Software Foundation* and *Open Source Initiative*. See *Resources* section at the end of this guide.

Caution - Do <u>not</u> use *Creative Commons* licenses for software source code because they do not address distribution of the code. See *Resources* section for when to use Creative Commons.

Because of this valuable resource, it's common for software developers to rely at least in part upon open source code instead of creating the entire software from scratch.

On the flip side, developers cannot transfer ownership of this code to a client because the developers don't own it in the first place. Both the developer and the client paying for development are subject to the terms and conditions of the code's open source license.

This is particularly important if the open source license prohibits sale of software containing the code. A client paying for development of software that it plans to sell will have significant legal risks if the underlying open source code cannot be resold.

Contributor License Agreement

An open source project may have several independent developers, each handling one or more parts of creating the software. Each collaborator should provide the project's owner with a signed contributor license agreement (CLA) so that the owner possesses the intellectual property rights needed to license the software to others.

Are Open Source Licenses Only For Free software?

Although open source licenses may permit you to sell the software that use the open source code, they typically also don't restrict others from taking the same open source code and selling similar software to others. In other words, your customers may become your competitors.

One common method for earning income with open source licensed software is to charge for packages that contain software maintenance, technical support, training, etc.

Trademarks And Open Source Code

Just because a software is distributed through open source licensing doesn't mean licensees can use the trade name or logo of the licensor if they decide to resell the source code to others.

For example, Red Hat, Inc. is a multi-billion dollar publicly traded company known for its open source licensed software. However, others cannot legally use the registered trademarks Red Hat has for its name and logo to distribute open source code without the company's permission.

Open Source Documentation

Software support documentation can also be distributed by open source license (e.g. a user's manual). This will be a different license than the one used for the software itself because the legal rights the licensee receives to each will not be identical.

In fact, one can use a non-open source software license (e.g. when charging for the software) but also use an open source documentation license for the related user support guide that's given away for free to licensee.

Chapter 4 - Public Domain Software

Public domain software is software the creator has given away to the public for use without any strings attached. The creator is dedicating the intellectual property to public use as one sees fit.

By dedicating to the public domain without retaining copyright ownership, the creator has eliminated the need to obtain a license to use or repurpose the software. One doesn't even need to give attribution to the creator.

In a software development agreement, any public domain code should be clearly identified so the client receiving the software has been put on notice there are no ownership rights to that part of the software.

By the end of the 20th Century, open source licensing became the preferred alternative to dedicating software to the public domain because it enables the licensor to exercise some control in how the code can be used (e.g. requiring attribution).

If you see software that's allegedly in the public domain, be skeptical and verify it is before using it.

Why?

Software pirates have been known to release bootleg software copies to the public under the guise of being apps in the public domain. You could still be liable for infringement if you use software under the mistaken impression it's in the public domain.

Chapter 5 - How To Create A Software License That's Right For You

Ownership, License, Or A Combination Of Both?

The first step in creating a software license is to determine whether or not a license is right for the software in the first place.

For instance, if you're paying a developer to create the software, outright ownership of the software is far more valuable than receiving a license from the developer. And if the developer is using other code by license, you'll want a license to use that plus ownership of unique code you paid the developer to create.

On the flip side, if you're a software developer, you want to be able to recycle your code on multiple projects for different clients. This means you'd want to license your code on a non-exclusive basis to each client instead of transferring ownership of it to any of them.

Of course, in many cases, this issue is negotiable if the price is right. One can expect to pay more for ownership than a license.

Multiple Licenses?

The next step is to determine how many licenses you'll need for the software. For example, let's say you're paying a developer to create software you plan to sell to the general public. Here are some of the licenses you'll want to consider to protect your intellectual property.

As Licensee

If you're not receiving ownership of the code, you'll need a license from the developer (typically in the software development agreement). If there's open source code as part of the software, the developer should identify which parts are and the related open source licenses so that you know your rights and responsibilities. Public domain code should also be identified if used because there will be no license (or other intellectual property rights) for that code.

As Licensor

Now identify who will have access to your software. They will need licenses from you for that access. Look at the popular license types in *Chapter 2* to get some ideas. If there's also open source code (See *Chapter 3*) in your software, you'll want to identify and comply with that license when granting rights to your licensee(s). Of course, if any source code is in the public domain, you may want to disclose that to the licensee(s) too.

If there are multiple licenses, they will usually include a EULA for end users. However, you'll probably have others, such as beta testing, evaluation, and resale licenses.

Define The Scope Of Each License

License From Software Developer To Client

The license a client gets from a developer should be tailored to address the needs of both parties. For example, a EULA from the developer to the client might be too narrow because it won't let the client resell the software to third parties.

On the other hand, if the developer is retaining ownership, the license the client should receive will probably be non-exclusive so the developer can recycle the code on other projects.

Other issues to address in the license include whether it is revocable, perpetual, and if there are rights to transfer, assign, sublicense, etc. (see *Chapter 1* for more examples.)

Licenses Granted To Others

For the license types you've decided to grant others (see *Chapters 2 and 3* for examples), identify the scope of each license using the characteristics identified in *Chapter 1*.

In some cases, it may make sense to use open source licensing for your software. See *Chapter 3 - Open Source Licensing*.

However, in many instances, you'll want to take your list of license types and the scope of each to a qualified software lawyer to prepare licenses that meet your unique needs.

License Theft

Don't "borrow" software licenses you find online and repurpose them for your software. That's like someone pirating your software. You risk legal liability for copyright infringement. For willful infringement, you could be liable to the copyright owner for $150,000 statutory damages per violation, attorney fees, and court costs.

Quick Start Checklist

_____ 1. Identify the types of software licenses you need as either a licensor or licensee.

Examples: EULA, beta testing, resale, etc.

_____ 2. Decide the scope of each license

Examples: perpetual, irrevocable, non-exclusive, etc.

_____ 3. Determine if you:

(a) Can use open source licenses (if applicable)

Examples: Licenses from Free Software Foundation and Open Source Initiative

or

(b) Need to have a software lawyer prepare the licenses for you.

Do You Need Help With Your Software Licenses?

If you aren't dedicating your software to the public domain or using open source licenses, you may need help from an experienced software lawyer to prepare your licenses.

Let's talk about your software licensing needs. Go to https://mikeyounglaw.com/appointments/ or call 214-546-4247 to schedule your phone consultation.

Just choose a day and time that's convenient and I'll call you.

Wishing you the best.

-Mike

Michael E. Young, J.D., LL.M.
Attorney & Counselor at Law

About The Author

Since 1994, Internet Lawyer Mike Young has helped business clients prevent and solve legal problems.

President of the Internet Attorneys Association LLC, Mike has a law office in Plano, Texas (a Dallas suburb), and also serves as a foreign legal consultant in the Republic of Panama.

Happily married, Mike enjoys spending time with his family, walking his dogs, and self-defense training.

To learn more, go to MikeYoungLaw.com. While there, be sure to subscribe to his complimentary newsletter where you will receive important business legal news and tips by email.

Rate and Review

If you have found this guide helpful, please post a positive customer review for it at Amazon.com.

Whether you liked the guide or not, please send me a copy of the review you submitted to Amazon because feedback is important for updates and writing new guides too.

Just email a copy to me at mike@mikeyounglaw.com and I promise to respond.

Thank you.

-Mike

Resources

Caution - just as technology changes quickly, so does the quality of service providers. What's good today may become a poor or obsolete resource tomorrow. In short, perform your own due diligence before using any of the following resources. Also note that each of these resources are listed in alphabetical order by topic, not by preference of the Author or Publisher of this guide.

Software Escrow
- Escrow Tech - https://www.escrowtech.com/
- Iron Mountain - https://www.ironmountain.com/
- NCC Group - https://www.nccgroup.trust/us/
- PRAXIS Technology Escrow - https://praxisescrow.com/
- Open Source Software Licenses
- GNU Licenses - http://www.gnu.org/licenses/license-list.html#SoftwareLicenses
- Open Source Initiative - https://opensource.org/licenses

Open Source Documentation Licenses
- Creative Commons - https://creativecommons.org/share-your-work/
- GNU Free Documentation License - http://www.gnu.org/licenses/licenses.html#FDL

Source Code Repositories
- Github - https://github.com/
- SourceForge - https://sourceforge.net/

SaaS Cloud Platforms
- Amazon AWS - https://aws.amazon.com/
- Microsoft Azure -
  https://azure.microsoft.com/en-us/

Mobile App Store Developer License Agreements
- Apple Apps -
  https://developer.apple.com/terms/
- Google Play -
  https://developer.android.com/google/play/licensing/

Disclosures And Disclaimers

This guide is published in print format. Neither the Author nor the Publisher makes any claim to the intellectual property rights of third-party vendors, their subsidiaries, or related entities.

All trademarks and service marks are the properties of their respective owners. All references to these properties are made solely for editorial purposes. Except for marks actually owned by the Author or the Publisher, no commercial claims are made to their use, and neither the Author nor the Publisher is affiliated with such marks in any way.

Unless otherwise expressly noted, none of the individuals or business entities mentioned herein has endorsed the contents of this guide.

Limits of Liability & Disclaimers of Warranties

Because this guide is a general educational information product, it is not a substitute for professional advice on the topics discussed in it.

The materials in this guide are provided "as is" and without warranties of any kind either express or implied. The Author and the Publisher disclaim all warranties, express or implied, including, but not limited to, implied warranties of merchantability and fitness for a particular purpose. The Author and the Publisher do not warrant that defects will be corrected, or that any website or any server that makes this guide available is free of viruses or other harmful components. The Author does not warrant or make any representations regarding the use or the results of the use of the materials in this guide in terms of their correctness, accuracy, reliability, or otherwise. Applicable law may not allow the exclusion of implied warranties, so the above exclusion may not apply to you.

Under no circumstances, including, but not limited to, negligence, shall the Author or the Publisher be liable for any special or consequential damages that result from the use of, or the inability to use this guide, even if the Author, the Publisher, or an authorized representative has been advised of the possibility of such damages.

Applicable law may not allow the limitation or exclusion of liability or incidental or consequential damages, so the above limitation or exclusion may not apply to you. In no event shall the Author's or Publisher's total liability to you for all damages, losses, and causes of action (whether in contract, tort, including but not limited to, negligence or otherwise) exceed the amount paid by you, if any, for this guide.

You agree to hold the Author and the Publisher of this guide, principals, agents, affiliates, and employees harmless from any and all liability for all claims for damages due to injuries, including attorney fees and costs, incurred by you or caused to third parties by you, arising out of the products, services, and activities discussed in this guide, excepting only claims for gross negligence or intentional tort.

You agree that any and all claims for gross negligence or intentional tort shall be settled solely by confidential binding arbitration per the American Arbitration Association's commercial arbitration
rules. All arbitration must occur in the municipality where the Author's principal place of business is located. Your claim cannot be aggregated with third party claims. Arbitration fees and costs shall be split equally, and you are solely responsible for your own lawyer fees.

Facts and information are believed to be accurate at the time they were placed in this guide. All data provided in this guide is to be used for information purposes only. The information contained within is not intended to provide specific legal, financial, tax, physical or mental health advice, or any other advice whatsoever, for any individual or company and should not be relied upon in that regard. The services described are only offered in jurisdictions where they may be legally offered. Information provided is not all-inclusive, and is limited to information that is made available and such information should not be relied upon as all-inclusive or accurate.

For more information about this policy, please contact the Author at the e-mail address listed in the Copyright Notice at the front of this guide.

IF YOU DO NOT AGREE WITH THESE TERMS AND EXPRESS CONDITIONS, DO NOT READ THIS GUIDE. YOUR USE OF THIS GUIDE, PRODUCTS, SERVICES, AND ANY PARTICIPATION IN ACTIVITIES MENTIONED IN THIS GUIDE, MEAN THAT YOU ARE AGREEING TO BE LEGALLY BOUND BY THESE TERMS.

Affiliate Compensation & Material Connections Disclosure

This guide may contain hyperlinks to websites and information created and maintained by other individuals and organizations. The Author and the Publisher do not control or guarantee the accuracy, completeness, relevance, or timeliness of any information or privacy policies posted on these linked websites.

You should assume that all references to products and services in this guide are made because material connections exist between the Author or Publisher and the providers of the mentioned products and services ("Provider").

You should also assume that all hyperlinks within this guide are affiliate links for (a) the Author, (b) the Publisher, or (c) someone else who is an affiliate for the mentioned products and services (individually and collectively, the "Affiliate").

The Affiliate recommends products and services in this guide based in part on a good faith belief that the purchase of such products or services will help readers in general.

The Affiliate has this good faith belief because (a) the Affiliate has tried the product or service mentioned prior to recommending it or (b) the Affiliate has researched the reputation of the Provider and has made the decision to recommend the Provider's products or services based on the Provider's history of providing these or other products or services.

The representations made by the Affiliate about products and services reflect the Affiliate's honest opinion based upon the facts known to the Affiliate at the time this guide was published.

Because there is a material connection between the Affiliate and Providers of products or services mentioned in this guide, you should always assume that the Affiliate may be biased because of the Affiliate's relationship with a Provider and/or because the Affiliate has received or will receive something of value from a Provider.

The type of compensation received by the Affiliate may vary. In some instances, the Affiliate may receive complimentary products (such as a review copy), services, or money from a Provider prior to mentioning the Provider's products or services in this guide.

In addition, the Affiliate may receive a monetary commission or non-monetary compensation when you take action by clicking on a hyperlink in this guide. This includes, but is not limited to, when you purchase a product or service from a Provider after clicking on an affiliate link in this guide.

Purchase Price

Although the Publisher believes the price is fair for the value that you receive, you understand and agree that the purchase price for this guide has been arbitrarily set by the Publisher or the vendor who sold you this guide. This price bears no relationship to objective standards.

You are advised to do your own due diligence when it comes to making any decisions. Use caution and seek the advice of qualified professionals before acting upon the contents of this guide or any other information. You shall not consider any examples, documents, or other content in this guide or otherwise provided by the Author or Publisher to be the equivalent of professional advice.

The Author and the Publisher assume no responsibility for any losses or damages resulting from your use of any link, information, or opportunity contained in this guide or within any other information disclosed by the Author or the Publisher in any form whatsoever.

YOU SHOULD ALWAYS CONDUCT YOUR OWN INVESTIGATION (PERFORM DUE DILIGENCE) BEFORE BUYING PRODUCTS OR SERVICES FROM ANYONE OFFLINE OR VIA THE INTERNET. THIS INCLUDES PRODUCTS AND SERVICES SOLD VIA HYPERLINKS CONTAINED IN THIS GUIDE.

Made in the USA
Middletown, DE
09 December 2020

26999244R00031